WEIRD

SEA CREATURES

Text by Sarah Lovett

John Muir Publications
Santa Fe, New Mexico

SPECIAL THANKS to
Dr. James Nybakken, Professor of Invertebrate Zoology, Moss Landing Marine
Laboratories; William L. Gannon, Museum of Southwestern Biology, University of
New Mexico; and Jennifer and Christopher Knight

John Muir Publications, P.O. Box 613, Santa Fe, NM 87504

First edition. First printing September 1992
            Second printing December 1993
            Second TWG printing December 1993

Library of Congress Cataloging-in-Publication Data
Lovett, Sarah, 1953-
    Extremely weird sea creatures / text by Sarah Lovett;
illustrations, Mary Sundstrom, Beth Evans. — 1st ed.
        p.   cm.
    Includes index.
    Summary: Introduces unusual sea animals, such as the two-spotted
octopus, Florida fighting conch, purple jellyfish, and fireworm.
    Softcover ISBN 1-56261-077-5
    Hardcover ISBN 1-56261-175-5
    1. Marine fauna — Juvenile literature.   [1. Marine animals.]
I. Sundstrom, Mary, ill.   II. Evans, Beth, ill.   III. Title.
QL122.2.L69   1992
591.92 — dc20   92-18383
                                          CIP
                                          AC

Extremely Weird Logo Art: Peter Aschwanden
Illustrations: Mary Sundstrom, Beth Evans
Design: Sally Blakemore
Printer: Inland Press

Distributed to the book trade by
W. W. Norton & Co., Inc.
500 Fifth Avenue
New York, New York 10110

Distributed to the education market by
The Wright Group
19201 120th Avenue N.E.
Bothell, WA 98011-9512

ON THE COVER:
As it outgrows its old shell, the Caribbean hermit crab chooses a
new shell by sight. If a shell looks interesting, it uses its walking legs
to explore its texture. Once an opening is located, the crab cleans out
sand and dirt and then backs its way into the shell. It exits and enters
several more times before deciding whether to wear its shell permanently.
Photo © Animals Animals

TAXONOMY CHART

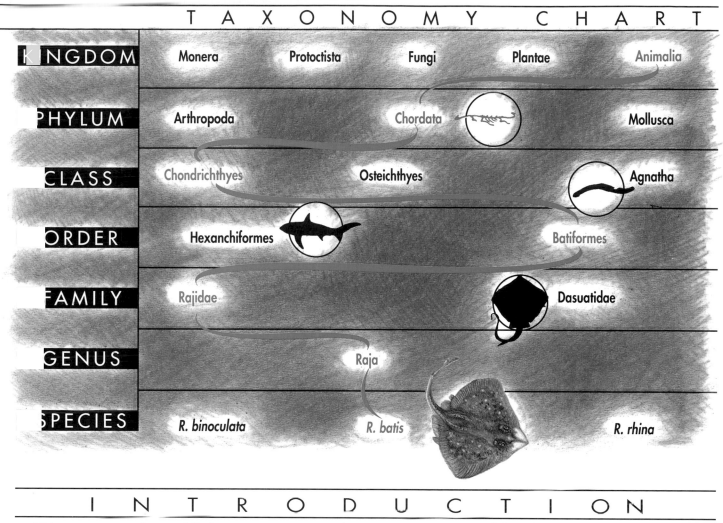

KINGDOM	Monera	Protoctista	Fungi	Plantae	Animalia
PHYLUM	Arthropoda		Chordata		Mollusca
CLASS	Chondrichthyes		Osteichthyes		Agnatha
ORDER	Hexanchiformes			Batiformes	
FAMILY	Rajidae			Dasuatidae	
GENUS		Raja			
SPECIES	R. binoculata		R. batis		R. rhina

INTRODUCTION

Oceans are the world's biggest ecosystem. They cover 75 percent of the globe. Although all oceans are interconnected, marine life and habitats vary enormously. The littoral is the land between high tide and low tide. Many animals live in this area where they receive a splashing tidal shower twice a day, and they could not survive on dry land or in the deep sea. Sunlit reefs support a vast number of animal species, including living coral, mollusks, and fishes who live nowhere else.

The water itself also provides a variety of habitats. Most marine animals live in the photic zone near the ocean's surface. Enough sunlight reaches this water so photosynthesis is able to take place. But some oceans are so deep, Mount Everest could be hidden under their waters. The deepest water is called the abyss. It is populated with animals especially adapted to zero sunlight, freezing temperatures, and intense water pressure.

Besides sea mammals such as great whales, porpoises, and manatees, oceans support marine fishes (the common skate, for instance), mollusks (like the two-spotted octopus), echinoderms (like the Gorgon's head basket star), and crustaceans (like the painted shrimp).

Sea creatures (almost all animals, for that matter) spend much of their lives struggling to survive—searching for food, a mate, and defending territory. They have evolved unique offensive and defensive equipment and tactics. Built-in spears, swords, lures, bows and arrows, nets, electric shocks, poison, speed, and camouflage are just some of the ways sea creatures defend themselves and/or prey on others. They also have unique ways of attracting mates and raising young.

To keep track of sea creatures and the millions of animal and plant species on earth, scientists use a universal system called taxonomy. Taxonomy starts with the 5 main groups of all living things, the kingdoms, and then divides those into the next group down—phylum, then class, order, family, genus, and, finally, species. Members of a species look similar and can reproduce with each other.

For an example of how taxonomy works, follow the highlighted lines above to see how the common skate, *Raja batis*, is classified. In this book, the scientific name of each animal is listed next to the common name. The first word is the genus. The second word is the species.

Turn to the glossarized index at the back of this book if you're looking for a specific animal, or for special information (what's an operculum, for instance), or for the definition of a word you don't understand.

FLIP MOVIE

COMMON CUTTLEFISH *(Sepia officinalis)*

If you had feet growing out of your head, you might be known as a head-footed animal. Of course, it would take more than that to qualify you as a member of the class Cephalopoda, or "head-foots." Cuttlefishes and their kin (which includes squids, octopuses, nautiluses, and spirulas) are grouped together in this class because they all have big eyes, pigment spots, armored jaws, and eight or more "feet" in the form of suckered tentacles that extend from their large head.

MARY SUNDSTROM

Millions of years ago, all cephalopods probably used the glands in their fleshy body wall (mantle) to secrete an external shell. Today, only the nautilus and the spirula have outside shells. The octopus has no hint of a hard shell, some species of squid have a trace of shell, and the cuttlefish has a limy shell inside its body called a "cuttlebone."

Like their relatives, cuttlefishes are energetic carnivores, and they prey on crustaceans. They have ten tentacles. The longest ones are used to catch a meal. Eight shorter tentacles are handy for grasping struggling prey, and the cuttlefishes' beaklike jaws easily cut through the shell or body of its victim.

Common cuttlefishes are found in the northeast Atlantic Ocean and the Mediterranean Sea. Other cuttlefishes live in other parts of the world, but none are native to North American coasts.

Cuttlefishes, write? Centuries ago, humans discovered that the dark cloudy fluid expelled in emergencies by all cephalopods to confuse their underwater enemies could be collected and used as ink. Cuttlefishes in the Indian Ocean gave the original "India ink" its name.

Cuttlebones, the limy internal shells of cuttlefishes, are sometimes hung in bird cages of canaries and other pet birds. Cuttlebones are a source of calcium; they also provide a handy place for birds to rub their beaks.

BETH EVANS

Photo, facing page, courtesy Animals Animals © W. Gregory Brown

SEA CREATURES

TWO-SPOTTED OCTOPUS (Octopus bimaculoides)

Although it has a fearsome reputation as a "devil-fish," the octopus is really an extremely shy, retiring critter, eager to avoid trouble—and humans. Usually, this bottom dweller stays out of sight in rocky crevices on lower ocean shores, scooting out of its nook in search of prey. When it is on the move, the octopus doesn't have a leg to stand on: it has eight of them!

The octopus uses its eight long, strong, flexible legs, or tentacles, to crawl along the seabed. Tentacles are also handy for building rock shelters and nests; the double row of cuplike suckers on each leg provides traction.

For a female octopus, tentacles and suckers are especially important. She lays her eggs in long strands and attaches them to the ceiling of her cavelike lair. She tends the eggs for two months or more, touching them constantly to remove dirt and fungus.

Like all cephalopods, the octopus depends mostly on its great big eyes to find prey (such as crustaceans and gastropods) and avoid predators. It moves very quickly once it attacks, enveloping the prey with its tentacles and biting with powerful jaws.

Octopuses live in oceans all over the world. The biggest of these animals has an arm span of 12 feet, although most octopuses are so small they can barely stretch across a one-foot circle. The two-spotted octopus lives along the southern California coast.

Smart guy! Although intelligence is hard to measure, scientists believe the ability to learn from experience, to evaluate information previously stored in memory, and to respond successfully to new situations are all part of being "smart." The octopus has a memory, and it is able to learn. In scientific experiments, these animals recognized and remembered different shapes by sight. They could also solve puzzles to find their way out of or into traps and mazes.

Many minis! Baby octopuses hatch fully formed with eight tiny tentacles and all their spots. Even before hatching, babies are able to change their skin color and squirt ink to confuse predators. Out of hundreds of eggs, only a few young octopuses survive to breed.

Photo, facing page, courtesy Animals Animals © Breck P. Kent

SEA CREATURES

ATLANTIC OVAL SQUID OR REEF SQUID *(Sepioteuthis sepioidea)*

In the Middle Ages, some naturalists believed that every land creature had a double living in the sea. Sea lions, sea horses, and sea cows, for instance, each had their match on land. So why not humans? Sea people, including a sea bishop, a sea monk, and a sea king, were commonly thought to dwell somewhere deep in the sea.

Squid are members of the class Cephalopoda and the phylum Mollusca (they're commonly known as mollusks). Scientists believe there are between 80,000 and 100,000 species of mollusks, and their fossils date back more than 500 million years.

All squid are deaf, but that doesn't stop them from chatting each other up. They do it with color. A blushing squid is probably trying to pick a fight. A spotted squid is saying, "Mate with me." And when a squid turns white as a sheet, the answer is "No!" Tiny sacs of pigment cells in the skin allow the squid and other cephalopods to change color.

Color isn't the only way a squid communicates. When it changes body posture, it alters the meaning of its message. Each squid has a very complex and compact nervous system in charge of this "quick change" communication.

Torpedo-shaped squid are extremely speedy swimmers, and they can accelerate using jet propulsion. They accomplish this by contracting their fleshy body wall and squirting out a high pressure stream of water. They steer by directing the water away from where they want to go. Some species of oceanic squid can propel themselves out through the surface of the water and "fly."

Squid are not lonely critters; they usually travel in large shoals (schools) when they are pursuing prey such as fishes and crustaceans. They spot prey with their sharp eyes and catch them with their two long and eight short arms that are equipped with suckers, some of them barbed. Their mouth has double lips and beaklike jaws—the better to bite with.

Unlike their kin, the octopuses, squid may bite when handled, but no cephalopod has ever been known to attack a human without being provoked.

SEA CREATURES

GIANT CLAM *(Tridacna gigas)*

Scallops, mussels, and clams have two shells, or valves, which is why they are known as bivalves. Although most bivalves grow only a few inches wide, giant bivalves can be measured in feet! One of these, the South Pacific's giant clam, has become well known through tales of science fiction and fantasy. While the real giant clam dines only on microscopic organisms, fiction has given this animal a sinister "man-eating" reputation.

A giant clam is not an aggressive predator, but it does have an efficient way to protect itself from danger. At the first sign of disturbance, it will close up like, well, like a clam. To do this, it uses its single, extremely strong, adductor muscle, which attaches one valve to the other. Could a giant clam trap a human diver? Not likely! Although the clam's muscle is strong, it is also sloowww, and it takes a long time for the shells to close.

While science fiction may portray this clam as a great gaping mouth, the brightly colored folds showing outside the shell are not lips. This overdeveloped filtering tissue provides living space for lots of tiny one-celled blue-green algae. While the algae snatch food particles from the clam, they also produce an oxygen boost (made from carbon dioxide, water, and sun) for their host. For both clam and algae, this is a mutually beneficial relationship.

Some scientists believe giant clams may grow to be more than 150 years old. Like trees, their age is measured in annual growth rings.

Heavy dudes. The largest giant clam on record grew 4¹/₂ feet long and weighed more than 500 pounds!

In the 1930s, a rough pearl was taken from a giant clam. It weighed almost 15 pounds (7 kg) and measured 9 inches (23 cm) by 6 inches (15 cm) by 5.5 inches (14 cm).

SEA CREATURES

The giant pink conch (*Strombus gigas*) may produce a 12-inch-long shell that weighs as much as 5 pounds. These shells are prized in Europe, especially in Italy, where they are used to make carved cameos.

FLORIDA FIGHTING CONCH (*Strombus alatus*)

A hermit crab outgrows one shell and house-hunts for another. In contrast, the Florida fighting conch is already equipped with a tiny shell called a protoconch when it hatches. As the conch grows, the lip of the shell expands, swirl by swirl. The original miniature shell can often be seen at the very tip of the massive adult shell. A shell provides shelter and protection because it is too tough for many predators to penetrate.

When a conch withdraws into its shell, it can close the "door" to keep predators out. This door is actually a lidlike covering secreted by the animal which is called the operculum. It is located on top and at the back of the conch's single foot. Although the operculum is often used for protection, conchs of the *Strombus* genus use it for locomotion.

Conchs are members of the scientific class Gastropoda, which means "stomach foot." Snails, limpets, and slugs are also known as gastropods.

A shell's shape depends on how evenly it grows. Growth occurs at the edge of the mantle as new lime is secreted. As the mantle grows, so grows the shell. If the lime is secreted evenly, the shell is a perfect cone. If the secretion is uneven, the shell has humps, bumps, twists, and coils.

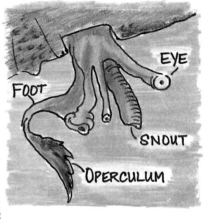

EYE

FOOT

SNOUT

OPERCULUM

Photo, facing page, courtesy Animals Animals © Zig Leszczynski

SEA CREATURES

BASKET SHELL (*Nassarius papillosus*)

This basket shell belongs to a group of mollusks commonly known as mud nassas because they prefer life in marine mud flats. Most species of the genus *Nassarius* are omnivores, which means they eat both plants and animals.

Basket shells, and most other gastropods, feed using the radula, or rasping, toothy tongue, located in their mouth. The radula is so sharp, it tears up tough food into digestible bits and pieces.

Some carnivorous (meat-eating) gastropods use their radula to scrape or drill holes in the shells of other mollusks, which are then devoured. Others prey on bivalves such as clams and scallops. When the unwary bivalve opens its two shells, the predatory gastropod pushes its snout between the shells so its extremely long proboscis (a muscular tube-shaped organ that contains the mouth, radula, and salivary glands) can be inserted.

The basket shell lives in Atlantic and Pacific waters.

In nature, there is a balance between prey and predator; one cannot survive without the other. For instance, sea otters prey on sea urchins. Without their predators, sea urchin populations would grow out of control, and soon they would destroy the kelp beds where they live. Without kelp beds, sea urchins would not be able to survive.

Quick getaway. Scallops (a type of bivalve) jet propel themselves through the water by clapping their two shells together. In this way, they shoot out jets of water from their mantle cavity.

Photo, facing page, courtesy Animals Animals © Scott Johnson

SEA CREATURES

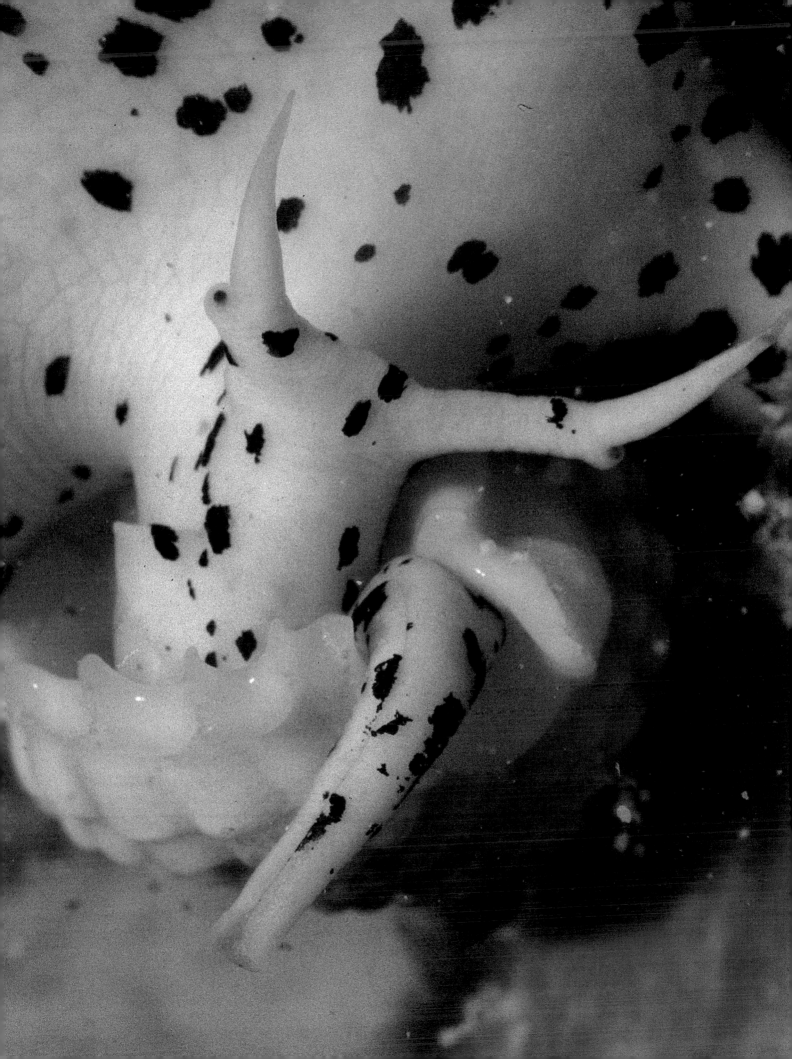

GREAT KEYHOLE LIMPET (*Megathura crenulata*)

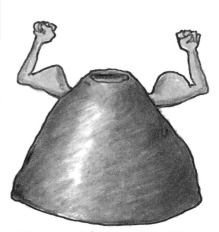

Limpets have one very large, muscular foot that has lots of sticking power, and some species use it to seal themselves to rocks. There, they rub a snug little hollow in stone using the edge of their shell and acid secretions. Although they move slowly, limpets may cruise as far as 3 feet (1 m) from the hollow. They travel in search of seaweed or algae to eat, but they always return to home base. If they don't want to move, they don't have to. Limpets cling like suction cups, and they can hardly ever be pried from their holdfast unless they are caught by surprise.

Some species are territorial and will staunchly defend their algae gardens from other limpets. They do this by wedging their shell under the intruder until it creeps away in defeat.

Most limpets choose to live on rocks near the ocean's surface, and they may be seen at low tide. Some prefer rocks in deeper waters, and a few attach themselves to large, floating seaweed. When they are in the larval (immature) stage, they have spiraling shells, but adult limpet shells are shaped like flattened cones.

The keyhole limpet has a hole, or "keyhole," at the top of its cone shell, and for this reason it is sometimes called a volcano shell. The great keyhole limpet is one of the largest limpet species. It lives along the Pacific Coast of North America.

Limpets stick to rocks with incredible suction power. In fact, their suction has been measured as 70 pounds per square inch of their foot surface.

The shells of dead (non-keyhole) limpets often have a hole in the center. These limpet rings are all that's left after the top of the cone is eaten away by a bird or bored into by a predatory sea snail. Limpet rings are easy to spot on beaches.

The limpet belongs to the scientific class Gastropoda, a group of snail- or sluglike mollusks.

Photo, facing page, courtesy Animals Animals © Steve Earley

SEA CREATURES

ATLANTIC WHELK *(Busycon canaliculatum)*

Whelks are univalves, which means their coiled shell grows all in one piece. They feed on the soft flesh of clams and other living bivalves (two-shelled mollusks), usually after prying both shells apart.

Like many other mollusks, whelks creep along on their extremely flat (and rather large) foot sole. They have a distinct head with tentacles, an efficient nervous system, and gills as well as a slime secreting gland. (Like land snails, whelks crawl on their own slime trail.)

Whelks have male or female reproductive organs. The female whelk attaches her eggs to ocean stones, and tiny, perfectly formed whelks emerge from the cases complete with miniature shell. (The female whelk pictured is depositing eggs!)

Whelk shells are made of calcium and other materials, and they only have one opening. As the mollusk grows, its shell enlarges around the lip and the opening gets bigger.

The Atlantic whelk is found along most of the warm temperate and tropical east coast of the Americas.

When you're beachcombing, look for empty whelk shells washed ashore. A window is often worn in the whirling whorl of the shell so the internal spiral pattern is visible.

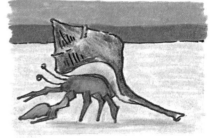

An empty whelk shell makes a favorite home for the house-hunting hermit crab.

SEA CREATURES

PURPLE JELLYFISH (*Pelagia noctiluca*)

The mythical Medusa had snakes growing out of her head, and she could turn humans to stone with just one glance. Jellyfish are also known as medusas, and like their namesake, they can paralyze with the sting of their snakelike tentacles.

Whether it is a giant red jelly (*Cyanea capillata*), 8 feet across with tentacles trailing 200 feet deep into the ocean, or a luminescent purple *Pelagia* (just about 2 inches across), true jellyfish are bizarre animals. They have been described as umbrellas, parachutes, balloons, blobs, and bells. Whatever you call them, their shape is often like a disk when they are relaxed and more or less hemispherical in the swim.

Since they do not have fins, how do jellyfish move about in water so well? If you guessed it takes muscle, you guessed right. Jellyfish have elastic fibers that help change and maintain their shape, and the main part of their body (the bell) has muscles running both radially and in circles something like the spokes of a bicycle wheel. Those muscles—lengthening and shortening alternately—produce the pulsating propulsion of jellyfish.

Jellyfish devour larvae, eggs, fishes, and whatever else is in their path. To do this, some species use the four arms that surround their mouth to sweep the water and gather particles of food. Others have branching arms with many sucking mouths.

Along with corals and sea anemones, the more than 9,000 species of jellyfish belong to the phylum Cnidaria (nigh-DAY-ree-ah), which in Latin means "stinging thread." These animals do not have a front and a back. Instead, similar parts radiate from an axis. They almost always live in saltwater, where some are free-swimming and others stay in one place. Either way, their tentacles are equipped with stinging cells that are coiled like tiny harpoons ready to fire by touch or a chemical signal.

The purple jellyfish, *Pelagia*, is found in open seas. At night, clusters of these jellies glow like white fireballs. Many jellyfish species give off light to attract prey or mates or light their own way.

Long, long ago, the jellyfish angered the King of the Sea— at least according to Japanese folklore. When the mythical sea king punished the jellyfish, he took away its shell and bones and had it beaten to a pulp; and that's a tall tale about how the jellyfish lost its shell.

SEA CREATURES

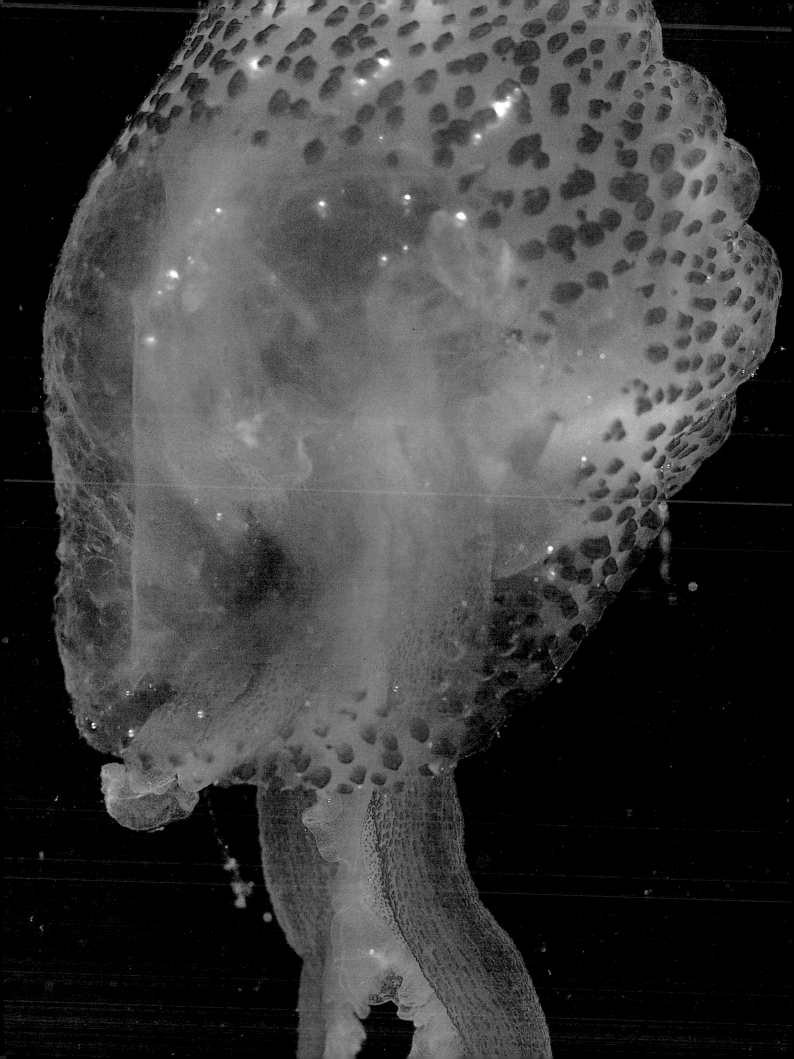

SEA ANEMONE (*Stoichactis* sp.)

Although a sea anemone looks like a flower (in fact, anemone is Greek for "wind flower"), it is a meat-eating animal. It uses its hollow tentacles to brush tiny animals or stuff crabs, worms, and fishes into its extremely wide mouth. The 1,000 or so species of sea anemones are polyps. They have a tube-shaped body. Their mouth and tentacles are located on the "oral" (mouth) end, while the opposite end is attached to a rocky sea bottom, seaweed, a jellyfish, or even a crab's shell!

Anemones are related to jellyfish, and like their relatives, they have stinging cells in their tentacles. They use these cells to sting fishes and other prey.

Like other animals, the sea anemone can sense chemical changes in its environment. When prey is near, the anemone waves its tentacles like many reaching fingers. If an unlucky victim comes too close, it is quickly popped into the anemone's mouth.

The giant *Stoichactis* anemone lives only in tropical waters, and it may reach a diameter of 3 feet. This anemone has a group of faithful crustacean and fish companions. Of these, the damselfish is the best-known. The anemone offers shelter for the fish, while the fish provides a cleaning service and bits of food for the anemone. A thick mucous coat may protect the damselfish from the anemone's stinging cells.

Melusine, a mermaid of French legend, disguised herself as a human and married a mortal man after he promised not to look at her one day each week—the day she had to turn back into a mermaid. Her husband broke his promise, discovered his wife was a mermaid, and Melusine went back to the sea. From that moment on, seeing a mermaid was said to bring bad news.

Photo, facing page, courtesy Animals Animals © Ashod Francis

SEA CREATURES

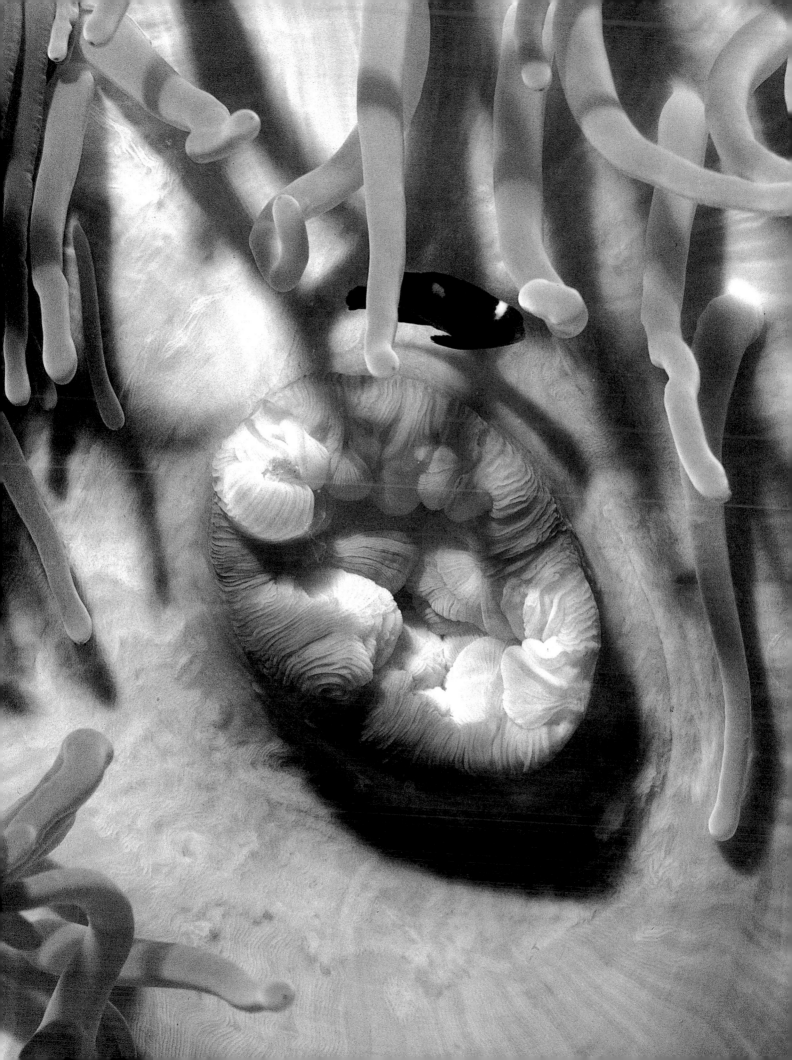

PYJAMA NUDIBRANCH (*Chromodoris quadricolor*)

A nudibranch, or shell-less sea slug, can take the sting out of a sea anemone's stinging cell! Well, almost. Most predators avoid anemones and their relatives because these animals have special cells in their tentacles that have the power to sting and stun. But some of the 5,000 species of nudibranchs are not bothered by stinging cells. In fact, they can eat them without harm and reuse them later for their own protection. The stinging cells pass through the digestive system of the nudibranch, travel into a special canal, and finally end up in the plumed gills (or cerata) on their back. When predators try to take a bite from the nudibranch, they get a sting instead.

Shell-less nudibranchs have other ways of discouraging hungry predators. Their body is covered with a slimy sour mucous that produces rainbows of color. The bright colors warn predators that nudibranchs taste bad.

Some nudibranchs have more tricks to ward off danger. Although they usually creep very slowly over seaweed, some species can actually swim. They twist their bodies side to side so their head and tail almost touch, and they stroke the water with their gills. If things get extremely dangerous, they can leave behind body parts that they regrow later.

Nudibranchs are hermaphrodites, which means they have *both* male and female reproductive systems, and any member of the species can mate with any other member it meets. They deposit clusters of eggs in jellylike bands. With one end locked onto a holdfast, the eggs look like layers of coiled fabric or gauze in a flowery shape.

Nudibranchs live in oceans from polar regions to tropical seas. The pyjama nudibranch (which does not have stinging cells) lives in warm waters all over the world.

Nudibranch larvae have shells, but adults have given them up to take an evolutionary gamble. It's working! While nudibranchs do not have the armor protection of heavy shells, they are more mobile and some can even swim.

Nudibranchs can detect light and dark, but they depend on touch and a chemical sense to find their prey. These carnivores prey on sea anemones, sponges, and bryozoans (minute mollusks).

Nudibranchs are colored by what they eat—literally. A scarlet nudibranch may be dining on a scarlet sponge. And the nudibranch who eats an orange sea anemone may have orange tips on its gills.

SEA CREATURES

AMERICAN LOBSTER *(Homarus americanus)*

More than 500 million years ago, ancient crustaceans roamed the shallow seas. Today, modern crustaceans (such as lobsters, crabs, and shrimp) are very successful ocean dwellers. These armored animals depend on a tough outer skeleton (exoskeleton) made mostly of chitin for protection from predators. (Mammals, in contrast, have inner, or endo-, skeletons.) In order for crustaceans to grow, the outer skeleton must be shed. This process is called molting, and it usually takes place once a year. Molting crustaceans crawl out of their old skeleton (they even leave behind their antennae), and their soft body quickly expands before the new exoskeleton hardens over it. Molting takes hours, during which time crustaceans are very vulnerable to predators. They will often hide in a crevice or under a rock until their new armor has hardened.

A crustacean's armor is jointed, and the limbs come in "right-hand" and "left-hand" pairs. There are sections of flexible skin at the limb joints, so the legs are movable.

To travel, lobsters walk on their eight legs or they swim slowly using their legs and their swimmerets (adominal appendages). They can also avoid danger with a quick thrust of the abdomen.

The American lobster lives in cold Atlantic waters off the New England coast and farther north.

That's swell! To crack open last year's cuticle, molting crustaceans swell up with water. After they molt, many eat their old, castoff cuticle to give themselves energy.

Many spiny lobsters are amazing migrators. At the first sign of winter storms, tens of thousands may travel in single file lines of 60 lobsters each, heading for deeper water. They will travel almost ten miles a day for two or three days!

SEA CREATURES

PAINTED SHRIMP (*Hymenocera picta*)

The tiny painted shrimp does indeed look like the creation of an artist's palette; it has a cream-colored body dotted with purplish-gray spots that are ringed with blue. Along with lobsters, crayfish, and crabs, this colorful critter belongs to the scientific order Decapoda, which means "ten feet."

The painted shrimp is active at night, and it dines only on sea stars. To do this, the shrimp may prop up and flip the sea star over and bore its pincers into one of the victim's arms. Scientists aren't sure why, but the sea star does not try to escape the shrimp. For several nights, the shrimp nibbles its victim until finally the arm is amputated. At this point, the sea star moves away, and later grows a new arm, while the painted shrimp continues to eat the old one.

A U.S. expedition discovered painted shrimp in the South Pacific in 1852. Painted shrimp are also known as clown or harlequin shrimp. Scientists count on scientific genus and species names to avoid confusing the many species of animals and plants that live all over the world.

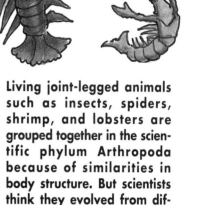

Living joint-legged animals such as insects, spiders, shrimp, and lobsters are grouped together in the scientific phylum Arthropoda because of similarities in body structure. But scientists think they evolved from different ancestors.

A cleaner shrimp? Some shrimp work as cleaners, removing parasites from large fishes such as moray eels. On the job, they may even crawl into the moray's mouth without fear of being eaten.

SEA CREATURES

SPIDER CRAB *(Libinia emarginata)*

Crabs and lobsters have pinching claws—the better to capture, crush, or rip their prey. These same fierce claws come in handy for defending territory, or for warding off predators.

While crabs wield their claws to escape danger, they also do without them in a pinch. Crabs have breakaway limbs—a special breaking point where the legs attach to the body. When an enemy has a crab by the leg, the leg snaps off, and the crab may escape. There is very little bleeding, and a new limb will grow in stages each time the animal molts its shell (usually once a year).

There are almost 50 spider crab families. Most are bottom dwellers, many are burrowers (who dig in the seabed to escape predators), and some swim using two legs as paddles. Like most members of its family, *Libinia emarginata* covers itself with tiny plants and animals such as sea anemones and sponges for protective camouflage. A well-decorated spider crab is hard to spot!

The world's largest crustacean is the giant spider crab *(Macrocheira kaempferi)*, whose name in Japanese means the tall-leg crab. This giant can measure more than 25 feet (8 m) from leg tip to tip! Its claws may be 10 feet (about 3 m) apart when it is ready to attack prey, but its body is only about 18 inches long and 12 inches wide. Giant spider crabs prey on other crustaceans and also echinoderms, worms, and mollusks—never on humans. The largest of these animals may live for twenty years.

Photo, facing page, courtesy Animals Animals © Breck P. Kent

SEA CREATURES

TUNIC (*Tunicate polycarpa*)

The tube-shaped tunicate or tunic is named for the smooth, see-through "tunic" that covers its atrium—the large chamber into which its intestine opens. Water is pumped into the tunic's body through a tube called the inhalant siphon. From there, it goes through the gills to the atrium and finally exits out the exhalant siphon. Its gills extract oxygen from the water, and they also filter out particles of food with hairlike cilia. Sticky mucous secreted by the tunic helps trap food before it is digested.

The tunic has no backbone, but in its larval stage, it does have a very primitive support system made of cartilage. For this reason, it doesn't qualify as an invertebrate (an animal with no spinal cord). Nor is it a vertebrate (an animal with a spinal cord). Instead, it is known as a urochordate, and it is closely related to vertebrate animals.

Some tunics are solitary. Others live in colonies. Grouped together, they look like colorful pots or jars anchored on the rocks.

Tunics are hermaphrodites: they have both male and female sex organs. They may mate with any other member of their species.

Tunics are also known as sea squirts because they squirt water!

Unlike their relatives on land, the seaweeds known as algae never flower, and they don't release seeds. Some reproduce by releasing sex cells into the water. Seaweeds are rootless, but they have many, many leaves.

Photo, facing page, courtesy Animals Animals © W. Gregory Brown

SEA CREATURES

GORGON'S HEAD SEA STAR (*Gorgonocephalus arcticus*)

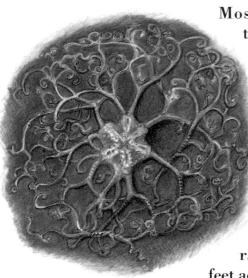

Most people look up when they think of stars, but down on the bottom of the ocean, thousands of species of sea stars can be found. Whether they live just below the tide line or 20,000 feet below the surface, sea stars (a.k.a. starfishes) are bottom dwellers. They come in a festive variety of colors—yellow, orange, blue, green, pink, red, purple—and range in size from 1/2 inch to 3 feet across.

Sea stars usually have five flattened arms that resemble the rays of a star. But close relatives of sea stars, the five-armed brittle stars (also called serpent stars), look more like exotic flowers or snakes than stars. Brittle stars are energetic critters, and they can break off body parts when they are disturbed. Later, they grow new parts to replace the broken ones.

Like all sea stars, brittle stars have a mouth on the underside of their body. They use it to feed on whatever particles happen to be on the sea floor.

The gorgon's head sea star is an extremely odd brittle star that is known as a basket star because its arms branch. The gorgon's head thrives in deep water, and its body may grow to be 4 inches wide while its arms branch again and again to a length of more than one foot each.

"Echinoderm" comes from two Greek words: *echinos* means spiny, and *derma* means skin. Starfishes, sea urchins, sea cucumbers, and sand dollars are among the 6,000 animal species who belong to the prickly "spiny skin" phylum, echinoderms.

Although, to human eyes, sea stars seem to go almost nowhere, they are not rooted. And because sea stars have an inner skeleton made of many flexible hinges, they are slow motion contortionists—they can twist into almost impossible shapes!

Photo, facing page, courtesy Animals Animals © Zig Leszczynski

SEA CREATURES

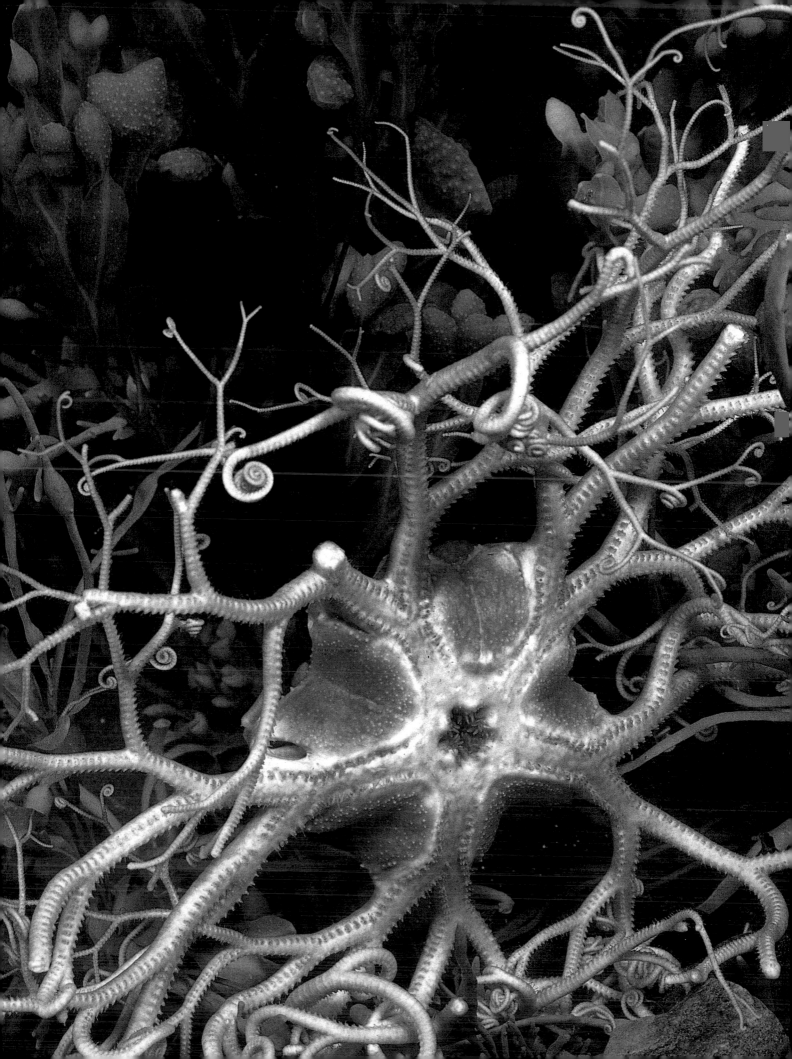

SLATE PENCIL SEA URCHIN *(Eucidaris tribuloides)*

The sea urchin is a very spiny critter. Beneath its many spines is a globe-shaped exoskeleton (outer skeleton) called a test, made of five plates that are hardened by deposits of lime. While the exoskeleton protects the sea urchin's insides, its outer spines help discourage predators. Spines are also handy to keep a sea urchin on the move. A ball-and-socket joint at the base of each spine is attached to the test by tiny muscles. These muscles tilt the spines and "walk" the sea urchin wherever it needs to go.

Sea urchins may also use their spines to burrow into rock crevices and to sting their prey. Many a swimmer remembers the painful sting of an urchin.

There are about 800 species of sea urchins, and they vary in size from two inches to one foot in diameter. The slate pencil sea urchin lives in the waters of the Caribbean and the tropical Atlantic.

Echinoderms are thought to be the invertebrates most closely related to vertebrates (like us!). Zoologists have studied the development of the echinoderm's embryos and have learned that their ancestors were similar to the ancestors of vertebrates.

Although sand dollars are fuzzily spined and flat, they are related to sea urchins. By the time sand dollars and sea urchins wash up on beaches, they've usually lost most of their spines.

Photo, facing page, courtesy Animals Animals /OSF

SEA CREATURES

SEA CUCUMBER *(Thelemota ananas)*

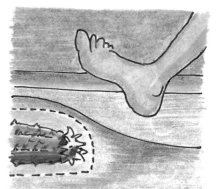

As the sausage-shaped sea cucumber creeps inch by inch, centimeter by centimeter, across the shallow seabed, it seems like a walking meal. Actually, when it comes to protecting itself from predators, the slow-motion sea cucumber has some very special defenses.

Some species have a poisonous skin to discourage hungry predators. If a predator persists, the sea cucumber tightens its muscles and squirts water from its body. An extremely upset cucumber will turn itself inside out and spew out its innards, including its reproductive and respiratory organs and intestines. The attacker is caught in a tangled mop of organs, and the sea cucumber escapes. It takes about six weeks before the sea cucumber is able to fully regenerate the spewed organs.

Sea cucumbers live in all oceans.

Sea cucumbers are also known as "water pickles." They are very shy critters who like to bury themselves in mud where they are out of a beachcomber's reach.

Wrinkled, flabby, leathery, and punchy as pudding, sea cucumbers are no beauties.

SEA CREATURES

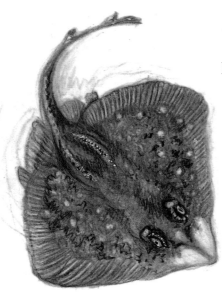

COMMON SKATE *(Raja batis)*

Rays and skates have a bad reputation, one that's really undeserved. Manta rays are known as "devil fish" and "devil rays," and many fishermen have superstitions about them because of their ability to jump out of water and land on boat decks. Stingrays are also feared because their whiplike tail is equipped with venomous spines. In a few stingray species, these spines can injure, even kill, humans, but they are used only for defense. Although rays and skates might seem frightening, they are generally peaceful, quiet animals who feed on plankton, fishes, mollusks, and crustaceans—never on humans! When threatened, they would rather flee than fight.

The biggest group of rays and skates is the Rajidae family that numbers about 120 species. These sea creatures prefer cool waters around the world, but they are even found in tropical (warmer) oceans at great depths. The smallest species, the little skate, grows to be only 20 inches (50 cm) long, while the big skate from North America's Pacific coast has measured in at 8 feet (about 2.5 m) and 200 pounds (90 kg).

The very large pectoral fins of many Rajidae species are often called "wings." Skates, such as *Raja batis*, use these wings to fly underwater with an up and down stroke that is so graceful it's enough to qualify them as underwater dancers.

The largest recorded manta ray weighed about 2 tons and had a wingspan of 22 feet!

Fishes are animals who have evolved for life underwater. The three main groups are bony fishes (such as carp and groupers), jawless fishes (lampreys and hagfishes, only!), and cartilaginous fishes (which include sharks, rays, and skates).

Photo, facing page, courtesy Animals Animals © G.I. Bernard/OSF

SEA CREATURES

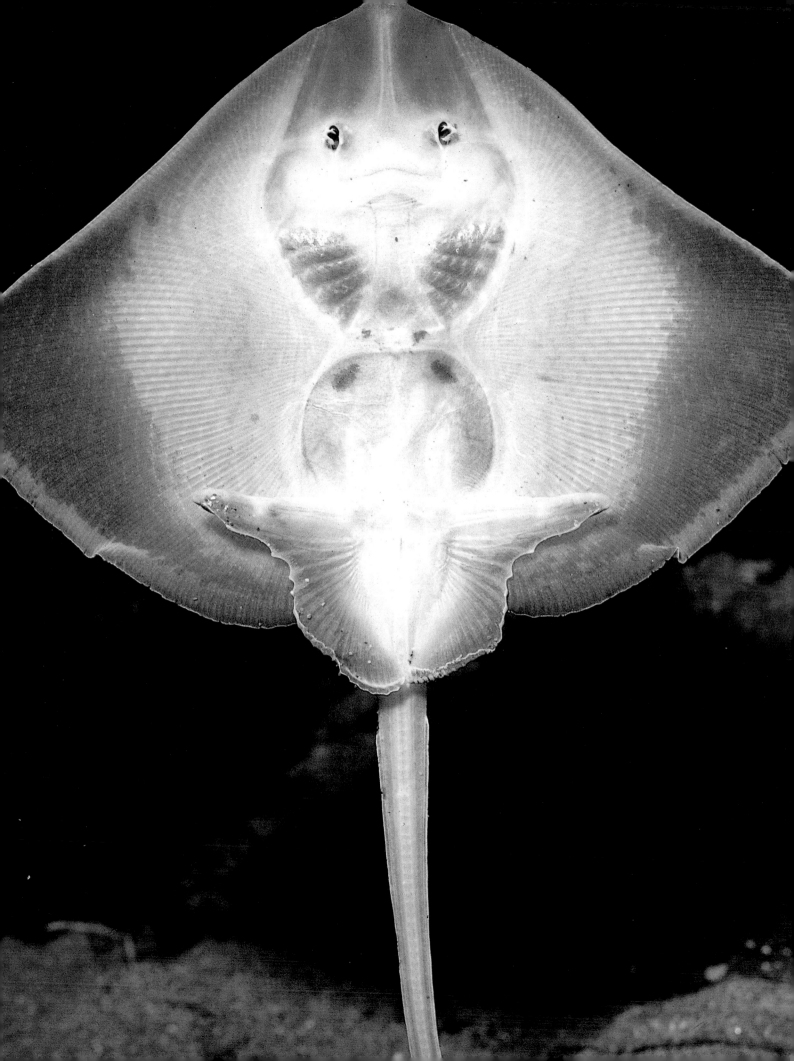

FIREWORM (*Hermodice carunculata*)

Female fireworms are flashy critters; they produce a substance that glows like—you guessed it—fire! When they are not glowing, fireworms are a greenish gold color, and their many parapodia (paired outgrowths from the side of each segment of the animal) are red and white. All fireworms have another hot trick. When humans or other animals touch the fireworm's thick tufted bristles, they get an "on-fire" feeling. This is caused by tiny poisonous, breakable hooks in the bristles.

Fireworms live in sandy Mediterranean seabeds where they create U-shaped burrows. When they are burrowed in, they wiggle their bodies to stir things up and to circulate fresh water. As the water passes over their gills, they extract the oxygen they need to live.

Fireworms are only one species out of 8,000 that belong to the class Polychaetes. All members of this group are segmented worms. Their long bodies are made of many parts, each separated by partitions, instead of joints.

Some fireworms reach a length of 12 inches!

When you're beachcombing, look for the burrows of lugworms. These animals live in U-shaped burrows; telltale signs include two holes several inches apart with a pile of sand next to one.

Photo, facing page, courtesy Animals Animals © Michael Pitts/OSF

SEA CREATURES

FEATHER-DUSTER WORM *(Spirobranchus giganteus)*

The feather-duster worm lives in a tube attached to a rocky tide pool or wharf piling where its tentacles hang out to "dust" the water for planktonic animals. Each worm builds its own limy home, and some tubes reach a length of 18 inches. Once the feather-duster worm has moved in, its large colorful, feathery plumes (which are outgrowths of the second segment of its body) are exposed.

Feather-duster worms are stay-at-home relatives of wandering fire-worms. They are shy critters, and some are so sensitive to company that even the slightest shadow will send their dusters back into the safety of the tube. They live in Caribbean and Indonesian and Pacific waters.

Seventy-five percent of the planet is covered by oceans. Pollution, overfishing, over-hunting, salt marsh destruction, and oil spills are only a few of the ways in which humans have had a harmful effect on ocean ecology. Remember that all life originated in the sea, and we still depend on a healthy ocean ecology for our well-being. Do your part to preserve oceans!

Photo, facing page, courtesy Animals Animals © W. Gregory Brown

SEA CREATURES

This glossarized index will help you find specific information on sea creatures. It will also help you understand the meaning of some of the words used in this book.